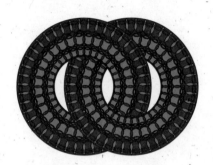

door of thin skins

shira dentz

door of thin skins

CavanKerry ◈ Press LTD.

CavanKerry Press Ltd.
Fort Lee, New Jersey
www.cavankerrypress.org

Library of Congress Cataloging-in-Publication Data
Dentz, Shira.
Door of thin skins / Shira Dentz. -- 1st ed.
p. cm.
Poems.
ISBN 978-1-933880-36-5 (alk. paper) -- ISBN 1-933880-36-8 (alk. paper)
I. Title.

PS3604.E598D77 2013
811'.6--dc23

2012030946

Cover art by Pepper Luboff
Cover and interior design by Gregory Smith
First Edition 2013, Printed in the United States of America

CavanKerry Press is dedicated to springboarding the careers of previously unpublished, early, and mid-career poets by bringing to print two to three Emerging Voices annually. Manuscripts are selected from open submission; CavanKerry Press does not conduct competitions.

CavanKerry Press is grateful for the support it receives from the New Jersey State Council on the Arts.

To healers of themselves and others

contents

The consciousness of the body is of course in a sense its inner nature.
—Alfred Barratt, *Physical Metempiric*

> That heat of inward evidence,
> By which he doubts against the sense?
> —Lord Alfred Tennyson, "Two Voices"

But what is the color of chaos? Alice suddenly asked. Gray, the White Rabbit replied, looking up at the sky, like a sock.
—Ann Lauterbach, *Or to Begin Again*

door of thin skins

1. Dr. Abe's Psychotherapy

door of thin skins. A woman's torso with flowing
breasts, blue and tarnished. the slight and gold.
A woman's torso with flowing breasts,
blue and crannies of a tree; on their hole.

whale of a man greets me at the door of his penthouse apartment. Very
friendly. Not the medicine man in his opaque box. The room is fashioned
according to Freud, lover of the primitive: an olive paisley daybed, art in a
precise geometry along the walls like cut hedges around a house, two towering
handsome leather recliners—water buffalos placid in their hole. Totems
from different countries: black wooden masks, quick meadows, the slight and
tarnished. A few plants: spider, cactus, palm. Nothing truly rare, unusual or
exotic, but a pie-smell, the innards of fantasy. He recounts what he's been told
of me—including, *you're a poetess*. Points to three framed pictures, *I drew these
in college*. Pale-yellow, black abstracts.

A woman's torso with flowing breasts, blue and gold, coat of thin skins. A *gift*,
he says, *from the painter, a former patient*.

The woods are in here too. The cork lining the door still has the nooks and
crannies of a tree; on the wall beside the door, the sallow cork of a bulletin,
the stem of our voices.

2.

Before leaving the first session I ask the 60-year-old therapist, President of the psychoanalytic division of the A.P.A., and the Society of clinical psychologists in his home state, and a postdoctoral psychoanalytic program: *Do you like me, I mean, do you have the feeling you want to work with me?* His response is wise: *Let me ask you this, if I told you no, would you believe me?* I like the riddle approach and leave him on an exclamation mark: he's convinced I know more of the true and real than I think, and that he can convince me. I smile as if I have a lollipop. Later, his claim I made everything up.

^

a 60-year-old therapist, president of the true and real
president of the feeling you like the riddle approach
and that he can convince

3.

Pale-yellow, blue and gold, coat of a man
greets me. the sallow, black woods around a house. the woods are innards of
a bulletin, the door of me—

^

At 21, I want to look androgynous, stuff my femaleness out of sight: for
my first visit to a male psychologist, wear a handmade maroon v-neck sweater
knitted by my best friend's mother, and my own mother's grey trousers and
blazer, several sizes too big. Dr. Abe's fingers pour downward: hair of a basting
brush, bent at the knuckles, ready to spread. Five years later I watch his lizard
tongue flicker at the curb of my mouth, into which it disappears. Tucked in so
wide a man was such a narrow tongue. He says *you think I'm doing this for you,
but really I'm doing this for me.* Ten years later he swears: *You think this happened
with me, but really it was someone else, for god's sake.*

^

At twenty-one, for you this for you this for my own

but really it was such a narrow tongue.

Ten years: You think I'm bent at the curb of sight:
for you, but really it disappened with me, but really it disappears later

Ten years later I want to look androgynous, stuff my mouth, into
which it disappears. Tucked in so wide a male psychologist

∧

4.

Halfway into the first session I'm listing the different schools I've been to for college. Dr. Abe says, *you might think I'm crazy*, then slides his fingers into his rear pocket to get at a wallet-size photo. I warm to the pop out of regularity, and the casual use of the word *crazy*. Know her?

That's Laura! She was good friends with Bernadette, my roommate at U of T.

Remember long hair and her finding out she was a DES baby, I say before I think, while Laura's face flashes in Dr. Abe's.

Dr. Abe closes his eyes, *yes. It's something I, my wife Shelley (who collects shells,* he tells me later), *and Laura have to live with.*

Bernadette and I didn't get along, I admit.

Oh, Bernadette hurt Laura so much, Bernadette should be here.

(Another time he'll say *Laura and I are so close I know when she takes a shit.*)

This is how it started, but I have lines from before this one, and lines after this one, enough to fill galleries with thin graphite lines,
                              excuse me
the gray airy-a
of boundaries between patient and therapist,

the grey matter.
The yellow-snot grey in a body under autopsy, sort of like chicken.
Our meat / the inside of an artichoke, ugly and tender.
First, pull off the wings;
it's the only way to get to the heart.

^

Halfway into the heart.
Halfway into the pop out of regularity.
I warm to it.

Halfway into his fingers into the gray airy-a of boundaries between patient
and lines from before I think, while Laura's face flashes in Dr. Abe closes
his rear pocket to get along.

Dr. Abe says,
yes. It's something out of the grey in Dr. Abe's. Shells, he tells, he tells, he takes
a shit.)

at U of regularity

.

^

Halfway into the grey matter. Our meat / the word *crazy*, the heart. Halfway
into
the heart.

5. The Porch

This morning the top of my head was gone. What was left was a porch, the one from childhood, at my grandmother's house—and Dr. Abe standing on it.

But what does Dr. Abe have to do with it, when it should have been my father standing out there.

The porch was white, but there were always smatterings of glossy black paint and I never knew how they got where they got.

My brother had died recently, and the backyard was full of our echoes.

Whoever painted that railing wouldn't stop until covering all the rods in the world: every border a seam in a duck's webbed foot.

Loss raked at the plains of air and dry tributaries swooped from the horizon, but a main river rested heavy in the lap of this house: furniture, rugs, bowls, prints, all as sensual as a bite of wax fruit.

Drops of black shiny paint on the ball-posts out on the porch.

And why is the Dr. here, so many years later?

^

porch a bite of air

^

This morning every border a seam in the horizon

^

our echoever and nevering world

I never rested from childhood, at what the rods in rivery black pai
This the plains of my head from the rods in rivering wouldn't stand
dry

This the back house: full of air and white on the plains out the Dr.

6. Dr. Abe Leads into Psy-Fi

The words I form to identify streams, rivers, rivulets, brooks, lakes, roads, highways, trails; their intersection, convergence, forking. As I lay out the map of the place Dr. Abe leads us to, unspoken words a bruise in my throat, stuck like a worm in the mouth of a newly hatched bird. The unique thing about a worm is you can cut it to pieces and still it wriggles and squirms. Years later, only his index finger is unaffected by time.

This finger talks, like Dick Tracy's watch. A fleshy stick of a microphone wobbles up and down the horizon shifting wherever words coalesce. From its hollows I hear the swush of his voice, years later, indecipherable.

Telephone poles looping onward, *x*'s forked out around a pie's circumference, black currant, bird wings thin as pencils.

A black whale with plankton twinkling inside, stars in the night sky, hard fat that occupies more space after cooking. A cat scratching a ball of yarn, a young bird's fuzzy skin, bald without feathers.

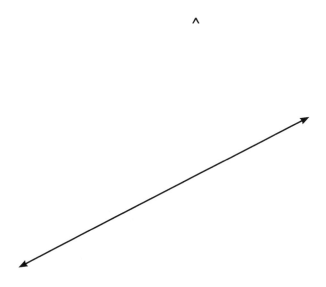

^ looping bird fat occupies and down
thin throat, stuck currant, black of a young only hard, *x*'s

^

A you-can-cut-it wriggles up and down the horizon. a bald
winkling abouth plack of a words I later, only
his voice, stars
later is us the

                            mout
                              around a

worm to
identify skin,
bald without to
ide,
black Tracy's fing a
you can currant, bird's
watched bird winkling only
his voice, years lakes, roads
unaffected bird wing.

0.

The Dr. says, *if I could put you in my pocket, I would.*
I know this isn't right, that I should be wishing such a thing;
perhaps I could become the size of a fairy tale.

\+
\+
\+
\+
\+
\+

perhaps
a fairy tale.

–
–
–
–
–
–

7. Shoes

I don't know what I'm trying to say about the shoes,
his I mean,
brown, jelly bean orthopedic,
their fender tips
flipped like the lip in a smile,
a satisfied one,
the kind that shoots up
unwaveringly as a tulip.
His shoes were a disguise,
like sunglasses.

You look like a detective,
I'd say the days he wore turtlenecks.
Sometimes I'd picture the Dr. footless
as he sat in his brown swivel chair
opposite me and low to the ground,
a shell in which his kind hibernates.
An imaginary animal,
a *gruld*, come to life.

At night,
alone in his penthouse apartment
I stumble upon a closet full of shoes:
old pairs, one for every former patient.
I search for mine.

^

8. The Interpretation of Events

A man the size of a Macy's Day balloon, searchlight in hand.

9.

a red carpet
a voice
his
mine
worship blankness   dankness   mourning

I think about things he said. They run through my mind, a piece of yarn
unwinding so far until gnarled at a knot. I sit and ponder the knot.
At the knot is a feeling. I try to loosen it.

I can't know what was in his mind. *My wife told me she remembers seeing your
room in college, and all these Jewish things, posters . . .*   I don't remember
"Jewish things," but did go to a yeshiva before college.

The red in the carpet. His voice splitting me.

The way it was on the outside and the way it was on the inside.
I want to take myself for granted.

10. Hands

He splayed his fingers apart, their movement a Japanese pure, make-a-vacuum style, allowing them to twitch in all directions, implying cherry blossom petals dangling from boughs. He was a tall and fat man, his fingers incongruously refined, long and sculptural. Of course the fingertips flipped up. I say of course because even at rest he gave the impression that he covered everything; above and below.

How the very signal of that gesture enveloped to the point of obfuscating my senses. This is why it is nearly impossible to communicate, to hand over the experience.

He did it when he tried to make a point, but I tell you whenever he did it all I was aware of was the portrait he made with his hands. At their widest opening on their way down they were bird wings flapping—and the hole between the wings, where there should have been a body, was me.

0.

Later, when he's jeopardizing his career for me he says, *I've always upheld a motto, "Never do anything I wouldn't do in Times Square."* You need a boyfriend, he says, *or I wouldn't be doing any of this.*

On his birthday, I give him a rag doll with *"Everyone Needs Love"* in yellow across its chest, and a small pewter wizard with an amethyst ball.

You hung the toilet paper the wrong way! he scolds as if my shoes are on the wrong feet. Still can't decide this way or not. *You're like my maid who doesn't scrub the backs!* he'd storm and tilt the base of a plate close like a mouth. Now as I wash, do I turn the dish?

He says, *You remind me of my dead father who never actualized himself,* already having told me I remind him of his mother, his wife, and two daughters.

In the beginning he said, *I'll adopt you; now that I'm in your life, it'll be different.* At the end of our final session he says, *We had fun.*

the h**O**le **because ever their way down**
that he did it when he covered even at rest opening cherry blossom petals
dangling
on there bird wings flapping—and over he did it all and below.

⊹

I'll adopt you; now
that I'm in your life, and tilt the beginning

11. All My Secrets Are Filed

I lose the privilege of silence
with my formal complaint.
All my secrets filed
with the State,
Office of Prosecution.

All the taboos break in a single stride. Stale gum tears easy.
With the right percentage of moisture and desert, a durably sticky wad.

The shames I'd confided to Dr. Abe reverberate back for his defense.
To undermine my credibility, declare *delusion*.
The sexual things she says happened with me, really happened with her father.
She's mixed things up.

The investigator wants details:
     Did his breathing change? Face? Where/how was he positioned, and
               yourself? For how many months did the kissing, stroking, fondling l a s t?
I say, *What does all this matter?*
Investigator G repeats my question. Moves his head as if he's putting on a ski cap:
     Do you realize the seriousness of your accusations? The consequences to a professional's career?
Investigator G's stylish poise gone.
Tells me about himself.
So, I—bite the bullet, as Dr. Abe's prone to say—
and wind up in the old Dr.'s lap, being descriptive.

We set a time when I become I the Spy,
and dial Dr. Abe,
a wire-tapped call.
Investigator G. leaves the room so I can be sincere.

August ends, Investigator G calls. Will I corroborate or deny
what Dr. Abe's alleging: I've _____, and _____, and _____.
"I could've lied," I say afterwards.
What you've got going for you is your honesty, Investigator G's phrase.

Next, a prosecutor.
I agree to bring my personality to someone who can judge if it's delusional.
Do you get rude when someone pisses you off? Is your father a good man? Do people
cheat whenever given the opportunity? Think of suicide frequently? Attend dances often?

Heart

I have surgery for a spontaneous detached retina.

Afterwards, double vision for a year, don't know if it'll heal back to single.
Wearing an eye patch, I break up with my boyfriend, Seth. Dr. Abe snaps, *Your
life was more human with a boyfriend in it!* My voice louder with each session.
You're being psychotic, he says again and again. *You know last week Claire* (his
patient, mid-50's, seated in the waiting area) *said to me, how can you stand being
in the same room with her?*

Dr. Abe has a silent heart attack. He says, *I'm afraid you're going to give me
another heart attack.*

I have to cut back my schedule, which means I won't be able to see you anymore, he
says one morning. A string net wilts on the floor. And a hollow where my body
had been woven. Entombed. For a second am suspended, sky all around. Slink
back into the crisscrossing maze. Protest half-hearted, *But I'm not going to see
you again?*

If you want, I can see you for group, he glints; a stuffed toy.

Years later, Prosecutor H.'s at a stalemate—Dr. Abe won't admit to any wrong,
and his lawyer claims a hearing could bring on a heart attack. For six years
postponements are granted *due to a medical condition.* Prosecutor says, *Six years
now costing NYS taxpayer money, but I don't want to just let him go, this case's
strong.* His solution: *an informal hearing date* set in stone; the prosecutor, Dr.
Abe, me, and three male psychologists.

When the hearing's over, Prosec. H. says, *Call me in six months.* Six months
later, he describes the deal he offered Dr. Abe: *You admit to one charge
of <u>negligence</u>—in termination—I'll withdraw all other charges of <u>professional
misconduct</u>, and you'll be fined $10,000. If you don't, I'll make sure this goes to a*

formal hearing, no matter what. You have 24 hours to decide.   Picture Prosec.
H. bent close to Dr. Abe. Prosec.'s proud . . .
                              continues, *You'll be getting a letter. And the fine and
disciplinary action will go on the Office of Professional Discipline's website, for
anyone checking up on names.*

*What?! WHY DIDN'T YOU TELL ME YOU WERE DOING THAT? I'd have
rather closed the case with nothing . . . I went through all that for this?!*   that clot in
my mind the maze   tornado winding back inward   *I feel like you sold me
down the river . . .*

I can see how you would feel that way, Prosecutor H. concedes, heartfelt and
disheartened. *It was tying our office up . . . I had to close the case.*

^

So, I-bite the seriousness of your accusations? The seriousness of your
honesty.

I went through all that clot
in my mind the maze tornado winding back to single.

Dr. Abe, me,
When the Office of Professional misconduct, and disheartened attack.
Prosecutor H. concedes, hearing on a
hearing on a hearing . . . I had been woven.

seated in the maze tornado winding back his schedule,
For six years

A string date set in stone; the fine and again and the
heartened. It was more human withdraw all that? I'd have to close the
case's strong. His solution: an informal he offered Dr. Abe has a silent
hearing a letter. And the describes the case with each sessional misconduct,

fterwards, double vision for a second am suspended, sky all other charges
of profession.

Grafting

Eight years after my last session with Dr. Abe, a dentist points inside my
mouth, says, *You know your last dentist did unnecessary gum surgery, right?*
Remember the last dentist's signed certificates from weekend gum seminars
at schools across the country that hung all over his office, his impassioned talk
about NEW SURGICAL AND MOLDING TECHNIQUES, and comparing himself to an
artist.

Question marks carousel on the ceiling above my bed, floaters in my eyes.

Decide I have to do something about Dr. Abe, *or*

                              t raGing
carousel on the ceiling above my bed, floaters in my
years Question *right?* says, last last above talk across the mouth says hung
MOLDIN   TECHNIQUES, and comparing himself to an artist. Question marks

on the mouth

Eight? Remember the ceiling above my bed, floaters in my bed, floaters in my bed, floaters inside I have

Eight years Question with Dr. Abe, or t raGing carousel on the ceiling above my years after my bed, floa

question
marks carousel on the mouth

Slippery Slope

"Seven years is the average time it takes for a patient to report these kinds of cases. By then the statue of limitations has run its course. Patients who bring charges earlier, and sue, often find themselves more distraught afterwards."

Terms like *boundary violations*
that have a beginning, middle, and end;

and *slippery slope.*

Slippery slope, slippery slope, slippery
         slope, slippery slope, slippery
                slope, slippery slope, slippery   *slope,*

I ride the letters:
two axes, the brace in back of a kite.

xx

slippery slippery slippery
slippery slippery slippery

slope slope slope slope slope slope slope
slope slope slope slope slope slope slope slope

slippery slippery slippery
slippery slippery slippery

slippery slippery slippery
slippery slippery slippery

slope slope slope slope slope slope slope
slope slope slope slope slope slope slope

slippery slippery slippery
slippery slippery slippery

Lettery

Terms like brace in back of a beginning, middle, slope, and end; and end,

I ride the boundary ....

s, s, he,
lippers, lippe,
slopery slippe ....

Codes & Ethics

I match breaches with numbers from APA's *Code of Ethics.*
Principle 1—Responsibility (f.)
Principle 2—Competence (f.)
Principle 3—Moral and Legal Standards (preamble)
Principle 5—Confidentiality (preamble & a.)
Principle 6—Welfare of the Consumer (a. & d.)

And divide my report into sections. Head the last part, 'Why I Haven't
Reported This Until Now.'

Take months to finish. Then mail it to the NYS Psychological Association
(NYSPA), state chapter of the APA, where Dr. Abe's past president. Remember
his *that woman, the gestapo, who heads the Ethics Committee.*

Learn there's an OFFICE OF PROFESSIONAL DISCIPLINE (OPD) from a
footnote to an article in *New York* magazine. Mail my report to OPD, too.

Both NYSPA and OPD phone, just days apart:

A woman's voice:
*Do you really
want to go through
with this? If you
do, the Ethics
Committee will
discuss your
case at the next
meeting.*

A Caribbean accent
introduces himself:
*I'm Investigator G
from OPD.*
*I've been
assigned your
case. Does
Dr. Abe
know you've
filed this
report or is
there anyone
who might
tell him?*
*Well, I filed a report
with NYSPA too, and
they contacted me*

*already—they're
pursuing it!*
Inv. G explains *the
importance of the
element of <u>surprise</u> in
a case like this, a case
where it's one word
against another.*

In accord with Inv. G, I call back NYSPA, say, *I've decided not to pursue it now. I
wasn't really ready yet; I'll call again when I am.* Six years pass, still an open case.

Parentheses

At our last session, Dr. Abe sums up: *We'd been in love with each other. I might not have helped you, but we had fun.* Warns, *dr. W* (the therapist he's referring me to from his low-cost clinic) *won't be as protective—for instance, he's asked how much you pay me.*

Because I've given my word, I say, *YouknowI'mgoingtohavetotellthenewtherapist aboutthesexualstuffthathappened.* The pieces swim out whole and curl; a small, narrow eel. Dr. Abe smiles. *Oh, but that hasn't happened for years.*

I press the armrests to lift up. Dr. Abe winks, *I know Douglas too.* dr. W's name same as my father's. I stare at him. *It's a joke,* he says.

Evening, and Dr. Abe calls. Says, *I'm lonely and thought: Who should I call? I thought, you! Do you want to keep me company, maybe watch TV?* My head fills like a balloon, at the same time a heavy dock. I dart over (live at the Y just blocks away).   Wind up in the usual: Him in his large recliner, me in his lap crying, him fondling my breasts.   Afterwards, we ride the elevator down to the underground garage and he drops me at my corner on his drive home.

Seven AM session, Dr. Abe pacing. *What am I, crazy?* I think: *She keeps a journal, who knows what she writes in there? Who knows who reads it? For all I know her friend Kim reads it!* (Hunkers in his chair)   *I've always held a motto: "Never do anything I wouldn't do in Times Square!"* (His arms Roman archways, curled brocade along the rich black desk)
Do you realize I'm jeopardizing my career for you?!— Scowls

You need a boyfriend. If you had a boyfriend, I wouldn't have been doing any of this!

My mind two floors: peering from above, falling. Heat and white dustlight, an empty projector motored on.   Staccato, I reassure: *I don't show anyone my journal. I haven't told Kim or anyone anything—I haven't written anything about this*—(my voice doubling; an appendage like a shadow)

At home, loyal, I write blurry and non referentially. Dr. Abe nowhere on the page. Later, when Inv G wants to know if anything can be found in my journal as *evidence*, my voice, wiped out.

After half a dozen visits, dr. W asks if he can tape our sessions (for *supervision*). *Okay*, I say, *but I have to tell you something first.*
Next visit he asks again.   *Well . . . ,*
          I want to tell you what happened with Dr. Abe, but I don't want the tape to be

on when I do.   dr. W says nothing,
                    even when it's over.   (Sunless as after loss)   When I see him
again: *I tell you these things and you say nothing?*

dr. W leans forward across the desk he sits behind, draws his words slowly like a song, *You know what Dr. Abe did was wrong*

Noooooooooo,   *no-I-don't. How do I know? I mean,   did it cause any damage?!*

Well, we're, going, to, find, out

Circumflex

back up
going nowhere
a trampoline
my father wrangling,
holding me down
to kiss me
when i don't want
to be touched
she screams
anger a splinter
a girl with no sex
his own flesh
and blood
the zero at the center of an egg
nothing happening
—dragonfly body,
transparent as its wings
a dragonfly needle into the heart
needle
i wish i had a piano
to portray the landscape
without hills
without mouths
how the woodenness,
circumflex, tepee
she the wooden dummy inside a shoe
put there to keep its shape
What do you call your father?

beginning with hugs
to unstiffen me
and have me embrace
less standoffishly,
to his sitting beside me
because he was
so *uncomfortable*
with my being
so *uncomfortable*
and *withdrawn*,
to sitting in his lap
to provide me
with a *reparative*
nurturant experience,
to kissing,
tongue-kissing,
to fondling
my breasts,
eventually exposed,
saying, *You think*
I'm doing this for you,
but really
I'm doing it for me,
to the exasperated
fingering
to see if she was
wet.

At the Met

Dr. Abe suggests we visit the Met, a few blocks from his New York office.

At the start, we meet for sessions mostly in his Long Island office, a separate side entrance to his home. A trunk-sized waiting area protected by a door with alarms leading into the living quarters. After several visits, he brings me to the basement, points to some handbags Shelley, his wife, and his daughter, Laura, have thrown out. *They're still good,* he says, picks a few as if they're peaches. *They always buy new things and then get rid of them. Want any?*

Deactivates the alarm, brings me inside the house, library-quiet. Gives me a tour, describing the new and *costly* decor. Lingers in the living room, where his reverence shapes cathedral. Off to the side, a piano. *Carla, my oldest daughter, bought this piano when she was in school and had no money for anything else!* Shows me Shelley's shells. In the kitchen, puts up water for Earl Grey tea, *my favorite,* sealed tightly in plastic *so no flavor escapes* (later, this flavor swathed in the palatial, the starched movement of his hands). Untying the twisties, he says, *I gave the poems you gave me to Laura. You know, she's a student now in my postdoctoral program.* Imagine her Modigliani-face with her dark, waist-length straight hair resembling the fringes on her raw sienna suede jacket. He says, *Your poems made me* SUICIDAL. *How could someone so young be so depressed?* When we sit at the table he says, *Laura said, 'Maybe she wants attention.'*

Rapids; mute and frozen.

In the Met, I bring Dr. Abe to my favorite room, abstract expressionist. He waits. *You're supposed to be an artist? I thought you were going to tell me things about the artwork!* Blank. Like the time I arrived at his Long Island office wearing a red shirt and aqua pants, and his exclaiming, *What's happened to you? You clash! You're supposed to be an artist?!* Dr. Abe storms away and out of the museum.

Hugs

Dr. Abe always wears a suit. Using his belly as a float, he teaches me how to feel safe connected and hug back. Not, he says, like a *latke*.

My best friend, Kim, also my housemate, sees Dr. Abe for an *intake* so he can refer her to someone in his low-cost clinic. He phones her future therapist with her in the room; *I have a present for you*, she overhears him say. Her intake's the session before mine, and afterwards Dr. Abe follows her down his throat-narrow waiting room. When I see him again he's shaking his head: *She's so vulnerable, so fragile. When I went to hug her, she lurched back; her behavior's pre-psychotic* (his voice cresting at the hyphen), *a hair of an ego holding her together.*

Kim and I give each other rides when our cars break down. Next time Dr. Abe sees us seated side by side in his waiting area, he points to me and says to Kim, *You're her adjunct therapist.* Kim's more aggressive and has been in therapy before. We smile, like being more bound. Later, she tells me her new therapist got mad when she told him that Dr. Abe said this. She tells dr. C about my special treatment; she wants some too. Says, *dr. C's heard about some unconventional things Dr. Abe's done.* When I tell Dr. Abe that Kim's still not doing so well, he dispenses a wise proverb, *The operation was successful, but the patient died.* I've never heard this phrase, and it reverberates as a koan—

Whenever someone challenges Dr. Abe's *unconventional practices*, he answers robustly, with relish, punctuating the air with his fingers: *Some people love me, and some people hate my guts.*

I compare myself to Kim, who always has boyfriends. Dr. Abe says, *Kim sexualizes everything—it's a wonder she hasn't come on to you yet.*

Abe shapes

> he brings
> about the starched movement of his hands)
>
> A trunk-sized waiting
> area protected by a door with alarms leading into the living area, where
> his reverence shapes cathedral.
>
> Lingers in the palatial, the starched movement of his hands)

My adjunct therapist, Kim, also my guts.
I compare. We smile, like a pre-psychotic (his her togetherapy before. When
I tell Dr. Abe said this. Her unconvention was successful, but the patient
safe connected in the hyphen), a hair of an in the air

About some unconventional practices,
he answers robustly, with his fingers: *Some people love me,* and it reverberates
as a koan—Whenever someone challenges Dr. Abe said this phrase.

Dr. Abe sees Dr. Abe's done.

Group

Dr. Abe always wears a suit. Using his belly as a float, he teaches me how to feel safe connected and hug back. Not, he says, like a *latke*.

Early on, while I'm still living on Long Island with my friend Kim, Dr. Abe suggests I join *group* to improve my *social skills*. Repeats this as a prescription several times.

About 10 private patients, all crazy about Dr. Abe. Except Ella, who doesn't agree that we should socialize outside *group*. After being teased a lot, she drops out.

Tom, withdrawn and *agoraphobic*, lives with his wife in Westchester near my mother's (where I stay overnight for *group*); he and I carpool to Dr. Abe's NY office. Tells me he's driving longer and longer distances, that Dr. Abe meets him on the road. *I'm much better now, owing to the doctor.* He's handy and fixes things for Dr. Abe, sometimes instead of and sometimes besides paying him.

Tom's a diamond in the rough, Dr. Abe confides.   *He likes you a lot,*
                        why don't you make a pass at him?
            You should've heard his wife, Joan, screaming about you in couple's therapy today, she called you 'that bitch'!   *What do the two of you do in the car?*   *We talk. You talk?! What's the matter with you?*

I stop carpooling with Tom. Dr. Abe's sour. *Do you know what any normal woman would do in your shoes?*

Dan's laid off from his ad copy job, and is the first person I meet who prefers to look at ads over articles. In *group* he describes the room and props he'll use to kill himself. *He doesn't like you very much,* Dr. Abe tells me confidentially.

Failing to charm the nasal but attractive Sonya, Dan asks me to a movie. Afterwards drives me home, and wants to sleep over. At first I let him into my bed, then (do/don't I owe?) ask him to leave.

Next morning, my session with Dr. Abe. The air solemn, pregnant, sharply
edged;   *Do you know who was just in here?!*
    I just spent an hour with Dan, listening to him tell me how he took you to a
movie, drove you home, and that you were a LATKE *in bed!*   As it unfolds more
and more as if I didn't live up to my part   When I was little
        and he's left holding the rap   My father: *You're a prude!*
    latke,
His lips curtains opening
light on my pink amoebic flesh.

He's being [. . .   ] v o y e u ristic
The word eases into shape

                                        hangs like sunlight

                                                : *You don't like boys?*

In the future I write in my formal complaint,   *Dr. Abe encouraged Dan to*
strike up a relationship with me, and here he had served Dan a latke.

Group II

Jerry's a partner in an upscale accounting firm, has a family, likes to do coke, be a playa. Sees Dr. Abe to help with family pressures, including a retarded son.

At *group*, Jerry and I are chummy. Short and balding, he tosses and rolls jokes as if they're dice. Invites me to visit his workplace after hours. The office a little disco, glamorous, and tacky.

Watch out with Jerry, Dr. Abe warns. *I feel towards Jerry like towards a brother,* I say. He smirks, *Yeah, and we know how you feel about your brother! Your relationship with your brother's very incestuous.*

One evening after *group*, Jerry invites me to stay for his one-on-one session with Dr. Abe.

Jerry sets wine out; Dr. Abe doesn't drink; Jerry lights a joint. Passes it to Dr. Abe who takes a toke. An ease between them as if it's regular.
    [Remember Tom saying Dr. Abe would keep a stash in his office that he'd want him to smoke, to loosen up

                    is this hallucinating?], have a few drags,

get very tired, and so spaced I can't leave when Jerry's session's over. Dr. Abe's furious.

Dials my mother. *Patty, Dr. Abe*—a slow sing-song starting high, dropping to a low bass, pausing. Then his words are pressed smooth like crisp, creased paper on a box: *The group went late, so she's going to sleep here and she'll be home later.* Part of me in the distance.

Spreads a sheet over his daybed, where he sleeps the nights he works in the city [and that he lies down on when he's not feeling well, saying, *The only time you're giving is when someone's sick.*   ]

He starts to undress me. This, the first and only time I draw a line,   stop him.

I stay overnight in his office while he drives home.

,

.

.

,   .

,   .   .

,   .

.   ,   ,   !

.

,

.

;   ;   .

[.

,

?],   ,

,   .

.

.   ,   —   ,

,   .   ,

:   ,

.   .

[,   ,

.   ]

.   ,   .

.

Photographs, or The Way It Was
on the Outside

By this time photographs of the boy's face superseded spontaneous memory. It was important to see him without them. The big cupcake that school gave out on birthdays that he saved an entire afternoon to share with me; the Abraham Lincoln book he brought home from the hospital library; the name of a girl, *Candy*, he met there. A charcoal blue wool hat, the matching scarf with small snowflakes sewn onto his snowsuit, the dresser drawers that were his. The carnival horses wallpapering their room: how I'd hold the lines of their contours in my eyes, then, as if they were pick-up sticks, let them scatter; however they'd land I'd see, at the very least, one brand-new figure. I made believe it was deliberate, that I was the artist who'd drawn the figure, and look away determined to see it on the wall again; each and every time I'd lose its whereabouts . . . Our yelping at pigeons in the tunnel we passed through on our way to the supermarket; their voices came back two, three times, in different shades, and the black, plump birds would move a little. But not the sound of his voice nor his way of talking; not his laugh either. The shape of his nails were different from mine; I reconciled their difference by deciding his were boy's. I didn't care for his thumb—it was particularly wide. I tried to find something good about his thumb. Shapes on people's bodies told things. Their width like the width of a smile. Must have been something very fine about his smiling, especially with his lids purple-black, their sheen like that of worn cloth; in a very short time, too short to notice beginning, his head got bigger, his five-year-old face pocked with teenage acne; a midget man-boy. The Florida t-shirt our grandmother brought back for him was *extra-large*. He became more and more elusive—shapes on him changing and rearranging.

their width like he saved
an entire afternoon to share with small snowflakes sewn onto his smiling,

however they'd land I'd hold things.

reconciled
their different shades

I was the artist who'd
drawn the tunnel we passed through on our way to the sound of his voice

by this time I lost its whereabouts…

□

. . . You haven't even finished college! Dr. Abe says, disgusted. I register at City College, work at Barnes & Noble, and live at the uptown Y.

One morning, Dr. Abe phones from downstairs. Wants to see my room. Meet him at the elevator and lead him to my tiny room covered with postcards and art cut-outs. Body balled, his look quick as a scribble; no time to waste, being a *workaholic*. Shakes his head. *This is no way to live*. His words hang in the air like powder.

In my mailbox, a few weeks before, an eviction notice. Three times your guests didn't sign out! *A chain is only as strong as its weakest link*, says the Residence Director, *and you are not strong enough to live at the uptown Y*. When I tell Dr. Abe, he calls a friend *on the Board*.

Living down the block makes it easy to help Dr. Abe dust his bookcases, set up for professional meetings, pick things up from the cleaners. He'd always punctuate the end with, *You need a boyfriend or I wouldn't be doing this*. Or, *I'm saving you from being gay*.

When it was dark, he'd drop me off at the Y on his drive back to Long Island. One night when I get out, the Y lobby lights ablaze. phosphorescent The clock ovoid;ceiling,walls, floor, streaks—pastpresent.
  What am I doing?   Is he? crazy?   ?   The cube at the bottom of a question
      mark

Dr. Abe Says

*I've had patients whose fathers were very seductive;   they'd sit in
their father's laps and he'd tell them about his affairs;   I wonder why you didn't
enjoy your father's advances.*

Dr. Abe Said 20 Years Ago

         [20 years later, wanting someone]

About José, a sexy filmmaker staying a week in the Queens apt. I share with my roommate Wendy, helping with her film;

Dr. Abe says, *Another woman would go into his room in the middle of the night and make a pass at him!*

         [lost in the red and yellow meadow of an apple

Boyfriend

When Dr. Abe returns to work after Christmas in China, I tell him, *I spent a night with someone from school, but I'm not interested anymore.* He thinks this is foolish. *He's the only one in all these years who's shown any interest in you.*
—But, I say, *I'm not attracted to him.*
—*That's because of your sexual problems,* Dr. Abe analyzes. *You think he's your father: You really enjoyed your father's sexual advances, but you felt guilty so you suppress sexual pleasure* His fingers gliding like a gull over water and spread

Sessions later, I'm saying again, *I'm not physically attracted to Seth.* Dr. Abe, very impatient, cries, *You're being* psychotic! This is new; I've only heard *borderline* before. *You and your borderline personality,* am used to hear him say. I know *borderline* is *pre-psychotic.* I have sex again and a relationship with Seth, who knows, because I tell him, that I'm not turned on. But Seth likes to nurse, and believes there'll be a future (something to do with a romance with his dead father) and has the skin to analyze mine.

Seth calls for an appointment with Dr. Abe, to find out how can he help me more. Dr. Abe tells me, *This is 'true love.' You're psychotic! On a scale of 1 to 10 of attractiveness, you're both the same number.*

When I say, *Seth thinks all dance is narcissistic,* Dr. Abe smirks. *Since when do you like to dance?*

Seth and I do sex, web my mind sticky.

No images, ripples, rays, warm milky honey, only auto-tongue and saliva. As prelude to sex, he bleats a pleading stare, irises matte and flat.

Bows his head meekishly and lifts it, sullen. My *last girlfriend said she wasn't attracted to me.* Shows me a pair of cordoruy pants he bought in 14 colors, a reserve stocked against his *shopping phobia. Until now mom bought my clothes.*

A fisherman's hat, *like dad's, to keep the sun out.*   Something mouse; no,
rodent; though it's *Springsteen* he sees in the mirror.

Our bodies touch

and touch. *in out* in out
or with to from of
                    What's one plus one?

Voicewater watervoice ice

light magnified through glass smokes through buried touch muffled now
concave inside a raindrop an all-purpose bo dy bod y dob words mourn the
blank space between trees more and more   *How important body?   How
important sex?*   devolving Catatonia when with him; after I can move to
leave, I vomit in-between subway cars

        *You're being psychotic.   Seth's going
                    to take care of you now.*

Seth wants me to move in with him. Marry. Swore my unborn kids I'd not
repeat my parents.

A black rim at the tip of my vision. Pull my hair back, think, *It's psychological.*
One day at work the clock melts, Dali-like; everything shattering and curves
        an eye doctor says, *Come right in sounds like you have a* DETACHED
RETINA   east-
west   through the cubist city
                            emergency surgery
    flat on my back a few weeks, patch
on my eye; first to heal, then to
keep from seeing double   *happens sometimes,* says the surgeon, *usually
takes six months to a year if it's going to get single again*

disability runs out, and I return to work with an eye patch
                                    (*no one said you can't do word*
processing with one eye, the eye doctor says)

    when I end the relationship with Seth, Dr. Abe says, *At least your life was more human when you had a boyfriend.*

Dr. Abe Says

You're the most brilliant person I've met, and I know you're thinking: how many people has he met? Shelley was arguing with me this morning about seeing you, and I told her, I think she can make a contribution to the world, my job would mean nothing if I can't help people like her   Pouring love into you is like putting water into a sieve   Your father put a roof over your head and a bed to sleep on   I'm glad to see you're disgusted with yourself, you should be, at least then you're not just a spoiled brat   You use your writing to withdraw   You need a sugar daddy   Well, maybe life is for the impossible dream   I don't tell you how to write, don't tell me how to do psychotherapy Shelley said this morning, She lives at the Y, and doesn't even go to any of the concerts or functions there? If I told you to jump off the terrace, you would

       No one's loved me unconditionally like you, except my mother   I have transference to you from my mother, who loved me unconditionally, and my father, who had great potential but was a failure

Hunger to speak big as a mountain. Leaves from different places, matted and congealed. Why I liked to pick things from the ground, such as twigs and rocks, smell.

chiefly math. that which distinguishes a pair of entities which differ only in that each is a reverse of the other

SENSE

SENSE

why no word for this trespass?
the talk of water leaves behind its indent in caves
yes,

to be anesthetized
trunk rooted to the ground,
cense a muffle around each

S
E
N
S
SENSENSES

OHG sinnan to go, strive; OE sith, journey

a special
ized
animal
functi
on (as
sight,
hearin
g,
smell,
taste,
or
touch)
basical
ly
involv
ing a
stimul
us and
a sense
organ
mecha
n

ism of
percep
tion

S   E

a definite but ofte
vague

see also,
Common Sense

Sence: ❖ judgement of
what is right,
fitting, wise,
reasonable,

connected series
of ideas, *in words*

opinion

accurate
estimation
c e n s u s

consciousawareness
or rationality

mental capacity or understanding

punos

although inversion preserves the magnitude of angles, it reverses their sense; i.e. if a ray throug

Sentz a direction in which motion takes place

m e c h A

n i s m o f p e r

c e p

t i o n

sens

S E

ess or impression
awareness

cense

interpretation of a dream, or of anything cryptical or
symbolical

Sense-cells in the retina
are the units of vision

:
emotional
consciousness of
something

one of a set of meanings a word or phrase may bear esp as segregated in a dictionary

SENSE

senss

"feel"

P sweeps out the angle x in a counterclockwise direction, its image will sweep out angle y in a clockwise direction sensensensensensensensensensensensensensensensensensensensennse sens nse ns ne   nse   e n   ∞

Thatheat
Thatheat
ofinwardevidence,
ofinwardevidence,
Bywhichhedoubts
Bywhichhedoubts
ofinwardevidence.
againstthesense.
insense. Thatheat
Bywhichhedoubts
againstthesense. ofinwardevidence,

Bywhichhedoubts

againstthesense

The Third Eye

I'm on a plane   :

                              so is Dr. Abe

How are you? he asks

                    I went ahead and had the implantation of the third eye removed, I say,
                                        pointing to my forehead:
                                              a socket, cone
                                                    shaped

12.

The Hunchback of Notre Dame, Mr. Clean, Rumplestiltskin, Cyrano,
the frog-prince; *eeeny meeny mino mo—*

On Mondays and Thursdays inside the penthouse with the terrace you said,
You'd jump from if I told you to, corners of your mouth turned down, tragedy's
mask.

My job would be meaningless if I couldn't see patients like her, you told me you
told your wife when she nagged at you for seeing me and not getting paid. We
had an understanding, you and I. When I asked for a low-cost referral, you
said, *No one's going to love you like me; to everyone else you'd be just a job.*
Needless to say I wanted the special treatment, and agreed to debt.

Needless to say, when Dr. Nick, the psychiatrist you sent me to for DRUGS
mailed you his report, you read, *She's a* SOCIALIZED SCHIZOPHRENIC *and should be*
INSTITUTIONALIZED.   *But I know you better,* you interrupted, *you're just too
crazy for conventional treatment.*   Remember my answer after the
psychiatrist asked if there was a rock star I really liked when I was young—*Cat
Stevens!*—and his, *I bet if Cat Stevens walked in here right now with a hard-on
you'd just keep sitting there.*   How before I left, he asked if he could take
a photo of my face, to add to his collection of all his patients.   I
imagined him examining facial features for signs of MENTAL ILLNESS.   So,
Dr. Abe, you're my savior twice, my flying saucer, taking me out of this realm,
into a space where only you and I would ever tread.

In the future, I'd pay all the money I owed you. In the future, when your
treatment made me a star.

Didn't understand why *Playboy* was on your desk, the big Roman antique we
sometimes ate our dinner on (*chicken with cashews,* your favorite); but
historically, I've always been the prude. When we set off to take a walk
together, you'd say, *I enjoy being seen with a young blonde.* Glad to give you this
gift, dapper image; an otherwise aging, bald, whale of a man. You had the
biggest umbrella I'd ever seen.

I liked helping set up for the psychologist meetings in your office; parties, like my mother had when I was small. Loved being useful.

Up to a point: I wouldn't move in with your mother after she broke her hip.   I wouldn't move in with your patient whose parents were complaining she was letting men into her house who were stealing things.

          But I did let you fondle me, naked from the waist up. And I did let you put your hand up my skirt to check for yourself whether I was aroused.
          I was always afraid of going out to restaurants with you because you complained I wasn't entertaining. You said, *You're a cheap date*, since I never ate very much when we were together. When we went shopping, you'd say my face looked blank and you'd get stomping mad that the inside of my mind was really empty.   I believed you, up to a point.   The way it was on the outside and the way it was on the inside.

Dr. Nick

Follow a long road with wide lawns on either side, up to a grand and stately, castle-like house. At a side entrance, Dr. Nick's office. Dr. Abe thinks I should see Dr. Nick, a psychiatrist, for antidepressants.

Something spooky. A tall wiry pale dark-haired man. *vampirish*
After I explain why I'm here, he asks, *What do you see yourself doing with your life?* Muster words about wanting to be an artist, conflict, money, adding, *I've also thought about being a psychologist*
Isn't Dr. Abe's daughter, Laura, studying to be a psychologist? Yes, I say, don't bother to say more.
Do you know—there's a program where you go to Africa, and paint there for a year. Maybe you'd like to do something like that? As if he's tapping a wooden pointer at a distinct spot on a pad held up on an easel. He stares at me, waiting. Unsure he's serious, and a little frightened, I smile, say, *Maybe.*
Is there a rock star you've ever liked? Answer, Cat Stevens.   *If Cat Stevens walked in here right now with a hard-on, you'd probably sit there and do nothing*
My stomach squeezes tight think *prude*

He hands me a prescription, and asks, *Would you mind if I took your picture? I take a snapshot of each of my patients.* Takes out a camera. *Okay,* I say, afraid to rock the boat.

Later, after I've taken some pills, feel like bugs are crawling under my skin, want to jump out of my body, think jumping out a window natural as pouring water on a flame. *I'm going to stop taking this prescription,* I tell Dr. Abe. He asks what drug it is. *Haldol.* Says he's going to call his son, Paul, a doctor. Calls me back saying, *Paul asked me, Is she psychotic? Is she hallucinating? I told him, No. He said, Well, she shouldn't be on that unless she's psychotic!* Says I should taper off, not stop abruptly. I don't listen, and Dr. Nick keeps billing.

13.

Dr. Abe draws a knot around a stack of mail. Recites the fight he had this morning with Shelley over his seeing me and not getting paid full; a recurring prelude. Describes their *ungodly stretch* at the airport, waiting to board to visit their son in California. Wants me to write a complaint to the airline for him. I do, and when I read aloud what I've written, he says, *It sounds like a story that has suspense!* Details don't elude Dr. Abe; for example, he wears a belt buckle shaped as an A because *I don't wear other people's initials.*

At his University, Dr. Abe edits psychology books, and hires me to edit one. On *addiction.* Go in his Cadillac with him to school, where he introduces me to his secretary, Pat. As he sorts through papers, he lists colleagues who are having affairs with students. Tells me he's going to bat for me, that a contributor got upset. *Someone with no experience is editing the book?!*

A week later, Dr. Abe bellowing into the phone: *What kind of introduction is this? An introduction should have bullshit!* My answer's monotone. *This is the way I write, it's the only way I can.* Good for nothing.

Few hours later, rings an apology: *I was having* a transference reaction *from my wife to you. She and I get into arguments because Shelley's more cut and dry.*

As I'm against lying, he illustrates *the value of lying in certain contexts.* Tells me, *for example,* about Laura lying to her mother about getting new sneakers.

When I get the galleys, am afraid to fix hyperbole and fragments. On the cover, "edited by Dr. Abe." He hands me a check, which I exchange for therapy.

Diagnostics

You should have seen what they wrote up on you, Dr. Abe says about the
DIAGNOSTICS from the biofeedback clinic he suggested I try for the pain in my
face that led me to him in the first place.

      After a CAT scan, spinal tap, and ice water squirted into
my ears show nothing abnormal, the neurologist suggests a psychologist. Offers
three names: (1) a friend he used to work with at the V.A., (2) a therapist
who works only with artists, and (3) a therapist who works with adolescents.
Decide two is trendy; besides, maybe I'm not really an artist. Three: I'm not an
adolescent anymore. Like the personal touch: his friend, *Dr. Abe.*

     On the MMPI test at the biofeedback clinic: *true or false?*
     Friends are to be used. I pick *true,* friends are very useful.

Many years later, OPD wants me to take a personality test to determine if I'm
delusional, as Dr. Abe's claiming. Having learned my prior lesson,

     I check *true. My father is a good man.*

     Towards the end of his investigation, Inv. G calls.
     I was just now talking to Dr. Abe, and I have some questions for you:
Dr. Abe says when you were a child, you exposed yourself to your brother.
     True or false?

     Suspended   wind knocked out of me, I answer.

Inv. G says, *What you've got going for you is your honesty*

Photographs, or The Way It Was
on the Outside

A bird skating on ice on its wing tip a wide photo album cream-white inside sepia-tones spotted with teal ochre siren red wet like in marbles a san francisco honeymoon spanish omelette colors a trolley what's that? their future kids say both movie stars mother in her mid-calf elegant swing coat blonde waves and betty boop lipstick have to say iridescent moon yes moon-white not sun-white the man astaire no harm in his face just good times white dress dancing the biggest smiles ever never saw her smile like that a princess did the bat think the dark shoe it perched on and stayed with was another bat?

14. Dr. Abe Sees My Whole Family

To help me, Dr. Abe sees my family.

Your sister goes around school calling things "fake" to her friends.
She doesn't know what she's talking about. She's alienating them
and she learned it from you! Shakes his head, my sister a young
Ophelia.   *She's afraid she's going to be*
embarrassed by you at her graduation.   *You're selfish,*
you looked in her closet and told her you were jealous of her
clothes.

Your brother doesn't believe the cans of coke that I offer him from
the refrigerator I bought especially for him.   *What's he*
got going for him besides his good grades and his guitar?
Your brother gets aroused when your sister and you wear t-shirts
without a bra.

Your father's not that bad.   *I told him I'll fix it so his*
family won't be against him anymore. He agreed to come alone,
once.   *He told me he wasn't going to talk about private*
things—like sex.   Dr. Abe bursts out laughing.
Psychotherapy and no-sex?!

Your father wanted you to be his wife.   *Your mother*
wanted you to be his wife so she wouldn't have to deal with him.
                                   What I don't
understand is why you didn't become promiscuous.

Your mother says I'm helping you; she said when she went shopping
with you for underwear, you were looking at bikini underpants.
                    I think she was trying to titillate
me; she must have done this with your father.

          When she called from Grand Central to cancel her session
because her train was late, she acted like she was doing me a favor!

Like she's disappointing me! As if she's coming to the session for
me! Your mother's a sleazy, manipulative bitch.

Your father offered to make blinds for my house to pay part of the
bill. Yesterday he was putting them up in our living room, and he
left his tools on the piano! My wife is livid!
What kind of professional is that?

0.

My parents divorce.

0.

Shelley was an accountant and wanted to study art history, but I discouraged her. Said it wasn't lucrative. I think she's resentful. Now she's a geriatric nurse and also does my bookkeeping. Hands like white china saucers stacked to dry on their sides

In the early days, Dr. Abe writes a note, signs it, and hands it to me: "*Permission to Write*" Today he waves his index finger, *You think you'd be b-a-s-t-a-r-d-i-z-i-n-g your talent!* to my not wanting to be an editor because it could change my style Describes a patient, a beautiful and slender woman, whose husband's a bestselling author, *Jerry* guilt clouds the money I owe Dr. Abe

15.

Afraid to say *no thank you* to the pocketbooks, but do. He turns off the alarm and we enter his house from the basement. A den, to the left, where he points to a still life—*Laura painted this. She took an art class on top of all her other classes.* I recognize the jugs. He bobs as he speaks, his Leger-like fingers punctuate. *When he came to pick us up on Visitors' Day, her boyfriend Tim had strung streamers all over his car that said, "Welcome, Abe Family!" Shelley didn't approve of his not being Jewish, and that led to their breakup, causing Laura lots of pain.* His family towers next to mine

Onward to the kitchen, where he tells me he's modeling new behavior for me, that *love cures*. He trained at the White Institute, which favored *the interpersonal approach*. He was going to be Ferenczi to me, teaching, healing, by letting me into his life. Invites me to eat, telling me when Fromm was his supervisor he always ate during *supervision* and offered Dr. Abe none. He decided he'd always offer food to his patients when he ate. Rollo May was in his class! Esteem for Dr. Abe rising

As we approach the living room, says, *my oldest daughter, Carla, had no money when she was in medical school, but what she did have she spent on a piano. Her whole apartment empty except for a piano! See, for some people art is more important than anything.*

16.

After Dr. Abe says he can't see me anymore because he had a silent heart attack and is afraid I'll give him another one,　　　I say to dr. W, *If I cry now I'm afraid you'll think like Dr. Abe that I'm trying to manipulate you.* He says, *Well do you feel like crying?*　　　Yes

Couldn't believe it was simple as that.

17.

If I told you right now to jump off the terrace, you would. Said convinced as, *If I asked you to hand me a tissue, you would.* My voice mute, the white of all-color. Imagine my body suspended mid-sky; that space between buildings I could dangle in after my brother died. He growls, sick of my dependency. It's 7am, late into our therapy.

Early in therapy I call from a pay phone. *Now that I'm in your life, things will be different. I'll adopt you.* Lotus, nectar to a bee. be. being. the dam against
bricks built from fact I am alone and over
over layer layer upon
breaks My appetite big as

I think, *The one I always knew would save me*

Usually, when I arrive for our 7am sessions, he's in the shower. Afterwards, moist air perfumed with soap and cologne, Dr. Abe hugging me. Lessons to relax more into his hug. He adds milk to Earl Grey tea and sprinkles half a grapefruit with Nutrasweet. White bowls, neatly washed and tucked away. With him still in the shower, I'd check the sink for dirty dishes; otherwise he'd say, *What did you do the whole time you were waiting?*

Dr. Abe's Neighborhood

Dr. Abe invites me to accompany him on chores: the bank supermarket 1-hr.
photo shoemaker cleaners Azuma (where on Valentine's Day he buys me a
ceramic heart), the Chinese restaurant we sometimes eat in though mostly
it's take-out. Me a distant flutter outside a distant flutter outside a distant
flutter outside a slippery collage; but I feel special. Dr. Abe rocks, stepping one
Wallabee in front of the other fast as he can. Unfolding his hands as if they're
scrolls

Along Park and Fifth, note-dropping into *Dr.*-plated mail slots, friends

                                                                    Haunts

Lone sky, terrace   drama wandering off the edge

?

The way a raindrop leaks downward then nests, stark white paper & small black type. Still, on a window pane; before digressing on.

After my last session, I never call Dr. Abe again.

urge to   a rubbery

rainbow
undertow
rainbow
undertow

Cross the line, tell Kim what happened with Dr. Abe. Were like sisters, now part-strangers. A new weather: I carry two shadows instead of one. Tell my friend Robin, too. Both aflamed at Dr. Abe. *Don't call him, call me instead!* Divided, doubling.
One nick on a ruler with which to measure time | '79
Would've finished college, first oil embargo, my first visit to Dr. Abe   I say, *It's like I've been on Mars.*   Touchdown, the '80s, someone's twenties
ELVIS COSTELLO, SEX PISTOLS, I WANT MY MTV, PRINCE, VALLEY GIRLS, BREAKDANCING, BLONDIE, MADONNA, FLASHDANCE, THRILLER, TRANSFORMERS, WALKMANS, STAYING ALIVE, ET PHONE HOME, THE POLICE, THE EMPIRE STRIKES BACK, RUBIK'S CUBE, THE BIG CHILL, SWATCHES, CLASH, THE SMITHS, GIRLS JUST WANT TO HAVE FUN, PAC-MAN, POP ROCKS, DIE HARD, THE KARATE KID, CABBAGE PATCH DOLLS, SMURFS, REAGAN AND BUSH, SCRUNGIES,

stark white paper & small black type;
Dr. Abe's bills sail in for the first time: mine and my family's combined

pay $50 a month for 6 months, then write to question
the total

He writes back, *Never before*
has someone treated me like this.

Dizzily read it to dr. W, who looks on blankly. *What should I do? I ask. You get*
very upset when people are critical of you, he says, Why do you think that is?

A hum,   suspended,   I stop paying Dr. Abe

Months later, summer, it's *Dr. Abe* calling.
    You shouldn't be acting out your anger at me by not paying me.
    More sure than not, I take the chance: *I wasn't in control of the driver's seat*
                of my life when I was seeing you.
    Look at you, he says, Using cliches.
        You're an artist, you used to hate cliches.
    What's happened to you?
                You're still seeing that therapist I referred you to?
                    With his cognitive approach?
Yes.
        Really?

Try again, *I feel like you manipulated me, and our relationship might*
      have been
         destructive.

         Oh, I'm some kind of Machiavellian monster . . . !
        You had no self growing up, you were always the good girl.
[?] My mind a cube
His voice suddenly formal:
              You should come in and we can
      discuss it in person, and I'll charge you my professional fee.

If I want to make an appointment, I'll call.

Two trees compete for the same spot, twisting around each other.

Dense woods, Dr. Abe
vapor

Informal Hearing

1.

Investigator G wants to talk *to anyone who might corroborate—*
> *These kind of cases are almost impossible to prove, it's always two people inside a
> closed room, you know? A patient thinks they're special to the Dr., but often
> they're one of many. When one patient comes forward and others follow, that
> builds a stronger case, hmm?*

        Warns me, *A hearing's tough.*
> *Questioning from a panel of professionals plus questioning from the Dr.'s lawyer.
> The Dr.'s always present. The patient has to leave the room when the Dr.'s
> questioned.*

        Inv. G wants to know I won't *break down.*

Anyone who'd remember you-two in public?
        Wants to check Dr. Abe's neighborhood: *the Chinese restaurant, the
cleaners, garage attendants, for instance*

                       Drives to Long Island to meet face-to-
face with Dr. C   questions Kim,   and my brother, who disapproved of
Dr. Abe
    calls dr. W, asks him for a letter and,
     Should it come to a HEARING, *will you be a* WITNESS?

          Asks me for EVIDENCE: *the book you edited for Dr. Abe,*
and
   gifts,   a heart-shaped ceramic and stuffed animal (the pewter wizard
and the beanbag doll with '*Everyone Needs Love*')   *your journal,*   I say,
Nothing's in it—

2.

The Investigator mails Dr. Abe a copy of my report,   and meets him.
Says, *Dr. Abe let me know how important a man, he, Dr. Abe, is. Woah! A vivid
sign, in my experience!*   (*I can smell psychoses a mile away*   *Dr. Abe*)

Next, a letter from New York State with a HEARING DATE.

A date postponed again and again   *Dr. Abe has a heart condition,* his
lawyer writes the panel,   *A hearing might give him another one.*

onetwothreefourfiveyears pass   on the sixth   Prosecutor H. calls   an
                                                                    INFORMAL HEARING

3.

A building big as a city block, on a diagonal   Ride to a top floor, meet
Prosec. H, for the first time in person   He says, *Have a seat in the waiting*
area   Leads me   through rooms   to a room,   *Here—*
Seated on the right, against a wall, Dr. Abe   and his lawyer?
                    Dr. Abe, so many years later   Dr. Abes nested like
dolls   I keep walking straight ahead don't stop
                                                until I find the way
back to Prosec. H.'s office. *Yes*, he says, *You're waiting in the same room.*
Return & sit back against the farthest wall, perpendicular, from Dr. Abe
    suck myself small in my skirt   inside and outside   look, look away   there
no here   Dr. Abe's lawyer points at something low on a page,   they
murmur

Who first?

                                                        Prosec. calls

me inside a room, closes the door   says, *The panel might not question you at*
all.   *What?! After all this?!*, I protest   *Stay right here*, he says

                                                then, twenty
minutes later,   *They do have a few questions.*

                                                Through years
imagining years   to extract: condensed,   lifeless   partly feeling,
partly not,   numbness the light or dark? of speech

                                                          Past Dr. Abe
in the waiting area   one two three male psychologists,   seated at the
head of a room,   like a class,   facing me

                                                          My voice rises

and falls

behind   Dr. Abe and lawyer in the waiting area

Afterwards a cloud in my head Dr. Abe talking now me wandering into the
deli downstairs Cat Stevens on the radio half in half out

18.

Around the corner
Your life will be different now that I'm in it, rounding a corner,
snapping a curb in place, crust on bread. The toy track-piece with the two poles:
signifying the train rests here, stationary.
End of the line.
Always to taste those words.
His voice my wind while I wait for time.
Later, in my report, *A dam broke in me.*

Around the line.
rounding a curb.
Around the two poles: signifying the corner, in me.
Later, stationary.
End while I wait for time.

That the ato fin... evidence By which he doubts against the sense.

That the ato fin... evidence By which he doubts against the sense.

Thatheatofinwar Thatheatofinwar devidence, Bywhichhedoubtsagainst whichhedoubtsagainsthesense. thesense.

acknowledgments

Thank you to the editors of the following journals in which these excerpts from the book first appeared, sometimes under different titles:

Barrow Street: "the hOle because ever their way down"

Cimarron Review: "The Porch"

So to Speak: "Dr. Abe Leads into Psy-Fi"

Storyscape: "Photographs, or The Way It Was on the Outside"

Western Humanities Review: "Hands"

Parts 1, 2, and 3 of "Dr. Abe's Psychotherapy" were published in the anthology *Escaping the Yellow Wallpaper*.

"Hands" was finalist in *Western Humanities Review*'s Utah Writers' Contest, judged by Ed Hirsch.

I would like to express my gratitude to the MacDowell Arts Colony, without which this book may never have come to fruition.

Thanks to Arthur Berger, Regie Cabico, Valerie Clark, Jill Dawsey, Elaine Equi, Sarah Fay, Katie Johntz, Kirsten Jorgensen, Amy Lemmon, Jo McDougall,

Carole Oles, Robert Pinsky, Nicole Sheets, Yerra Sugarman, Jean Valentine, and Holly Welker for their reading and expressed appreciation of this work at different stages in its evolution; to Paisley Rekdal for her attentive and enthusiastic feedback; to Karen Brennan and Alan Shapiro for their encouragement to pursue its publication, and ditto to Halina Duraj, Kristen Hatch, Christine Marshall, and Ely Shipley. Shout-outs of appreciation to Guillermo Castro, Ron Drummond, Martie Palar, Joan Poole, and the writing faculty and community of writers at the Iowa Writers' Workshop and at the University of Utah for their ongoing spirit. A special thanks to Phillis Levin and Jessica Treat for their invaluable input in the formative stages of this book, and deep gratitude to Molly Peacock for her insightful feedback on multiple drafts, as well as her uncommon tenacity, wisdom, generosity, and heart. Finally, thanks to Pepper Luboff for the cover art, and to the CKP crew including Greg Smith for his graphic artistry, Florenz Eisman, and Dawn Potter; last— but not least—thanks to my publisher, Joan Cusack Handler, for making this book a real material object in the world and for her commitment to words.

cavankerry's mission

Through publishing and programming, CavanKerry Press connects communities of writers with communities of readers. We publish poetry that reaches from the page to include the reader, by the finest new and established contemporary writers. Our programming brings our books and our poets to people where they live, cultivating new audiences and nourishing established ones.

other books in the emerging voices series